Maria Diaz

CROSS STITCH MOTIF SERIES 6

KITCHEN
180 NEW CROSS STITCH MODELS

TUVA

Tuva Publishing
www.tuvayayincilik.com

Address: Merkez Mah. Çavuşbaşı Cad. No:71
Çekmeköy / Istanbul 34782 - TURKEY
Tel: 9 0216 642 62 62

Cross Stitch Motif Series 6 / Kitchen

First Print: 2013 / March - Istanbul
Second Print: 2013 / May - Istanbul
Third Print: 2014 / September - Istanbul

All Global Copyrights Belongs To
Tuva Tekstil San. ve Dış Tic. Ltd. Şti.

Content: Cross Stitch

Editor in Chief: Ayhan DEMİRPEHLİVAN
Project Editor: Kader DEMİRPEHLİVAN
Designer: Maria DIAZ
Technical Advisor: K. Leyla ARAS
Graphic Design: Ömer ALP, Büşra ESER
Asistant: Kevser BAYRAKÇI

ISBN: 978-605-5647-42-1

Printing House
Bilnet Matbaacılık - Biltur Yayın ve Hizmet A.Ş. Dudullu
Organize Sanayi Bölgesi 1. Cadde No:16 - Ümraniye - Istanbul / Turkey

 twitter.com/TuvaYayincilik

facebook.com/TuvaYayincilik

 pinterest.com/TuvaPublishing

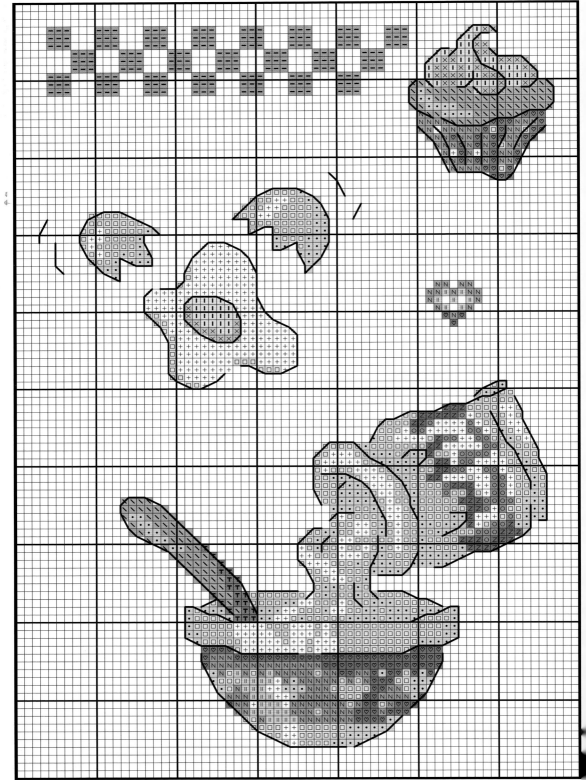

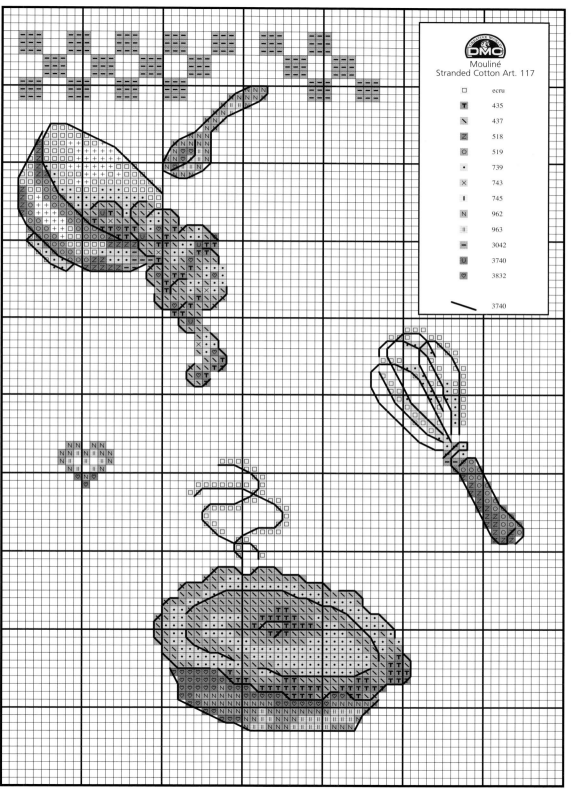

DMC
Mouliné
Stranded Cotton Art. 117

□	ecru
T	435
\	437
Z	518
O	519
·	739
×	743
I	745
N	962
II	963
—	3042
U	3740
♡	3832
╱	3740

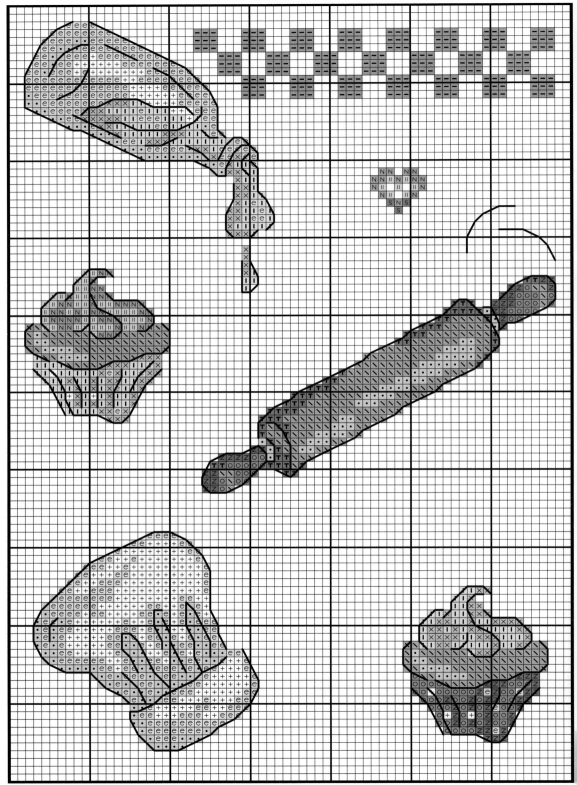

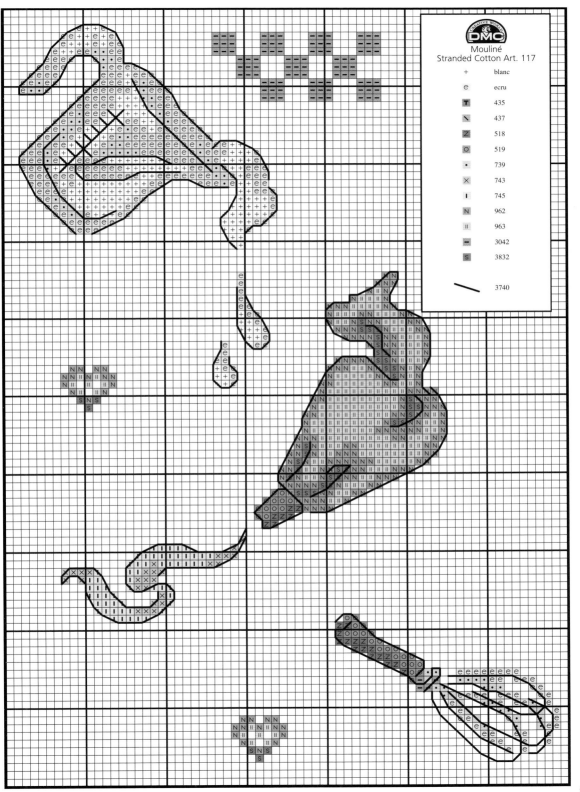

DMC
CREATIVE WORLD
Mouliné
Stranded Cotton Art. 117

Symbol	Colour
+	blanc
e	ecru
T	435
⟍	437
Z	518
O	519
•	739
X	743
I	745
N	962
II	963
‒	3042
S	3832
╱	3740

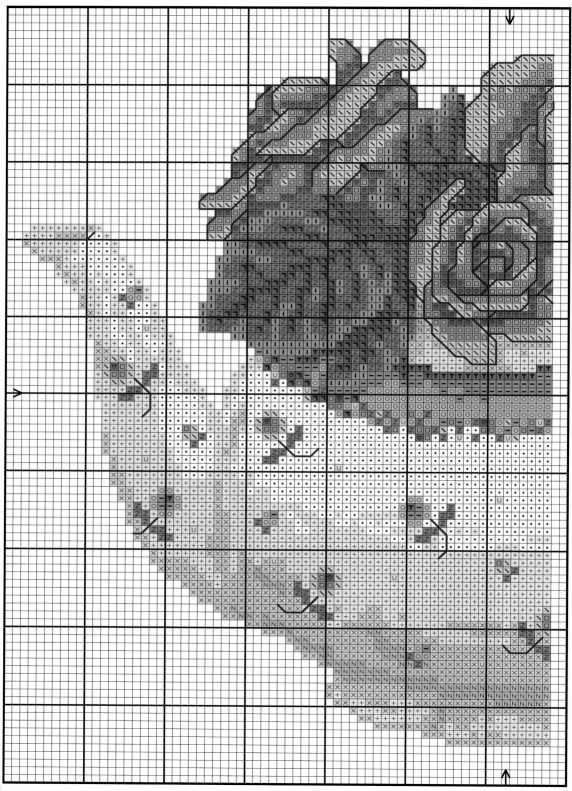

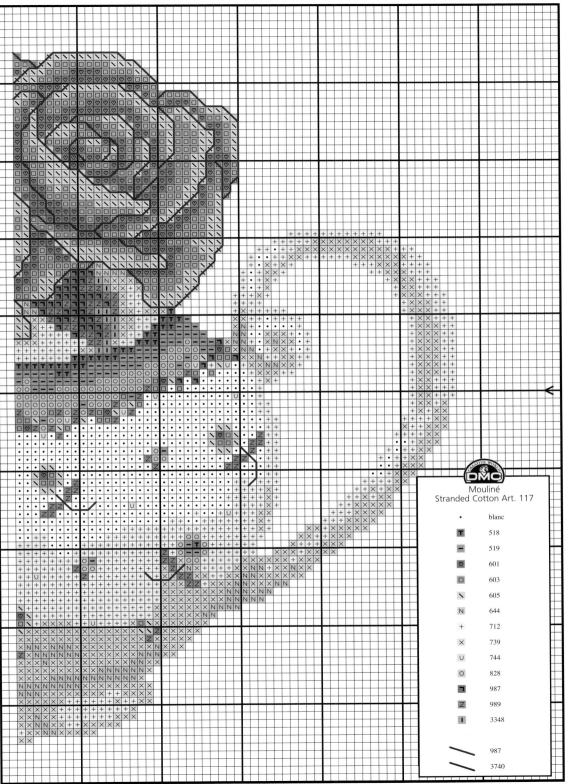

Mouliné
Stranded Cotton Art. 117

•	blanc
T	518
−	519
♥	601
□	603
\	605
N	644
+	712
×	739
U	744
O	828
⊓	987
Z	989
I	3348
╱	987
╱	3740

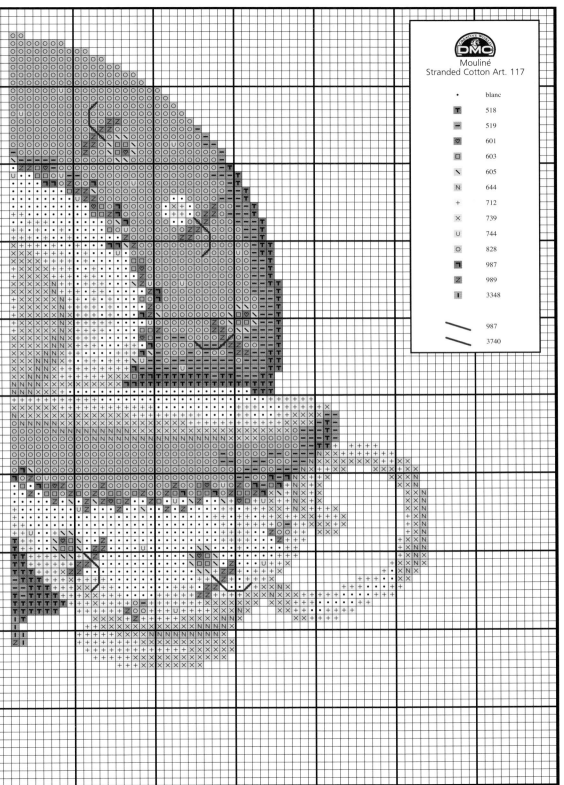

•	blanc
T	518
−	519
♥	601
□	603
\	605
N	644
+	712
×	739
U	744
O	828
˥	987
Z	989
I	3348
/	987
/	3740

Mouliné
Stranded Cotton Art. 117

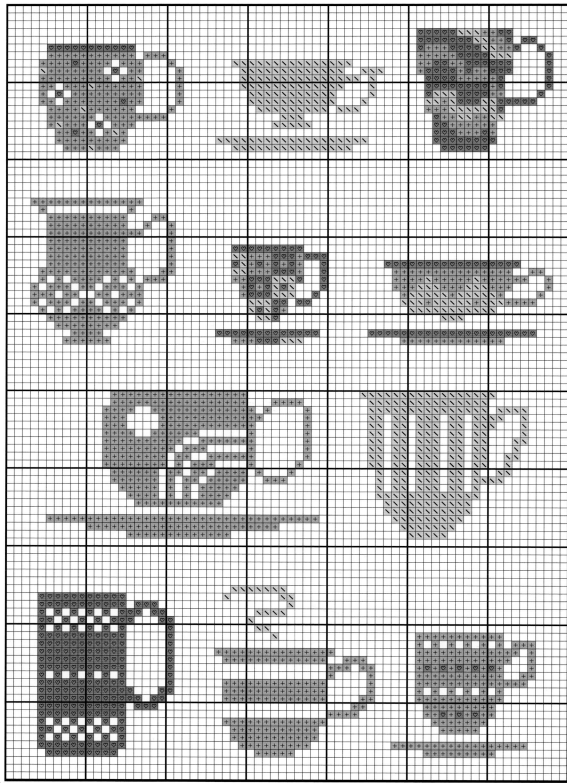

Mouliné
Stranded Cotton Art. 117

•	E3821
✕	304
▬	791
+	794
S	815
○	3807

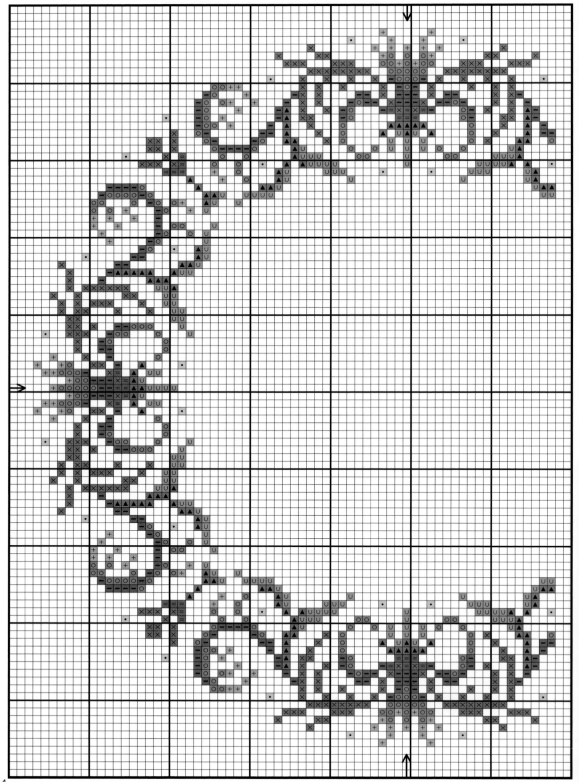

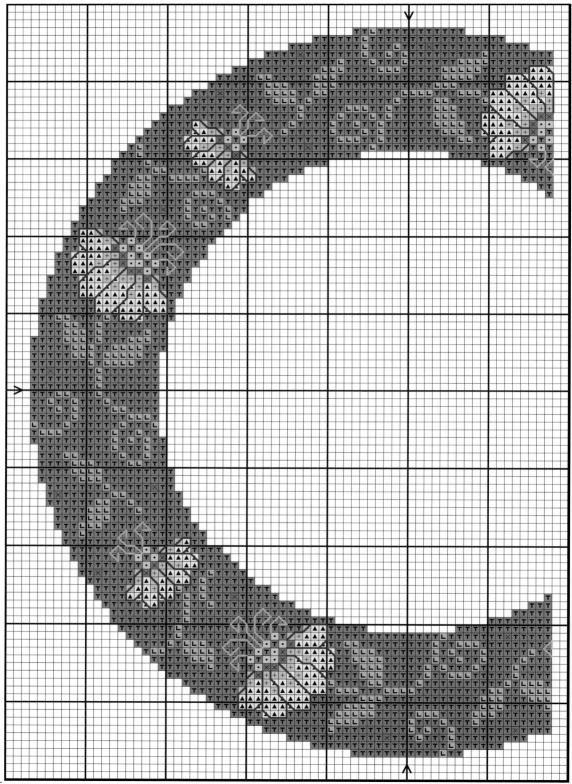

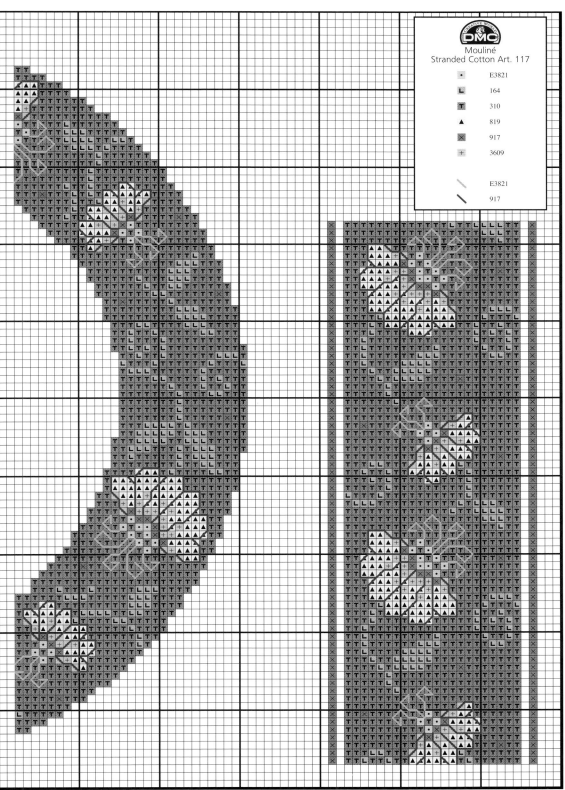

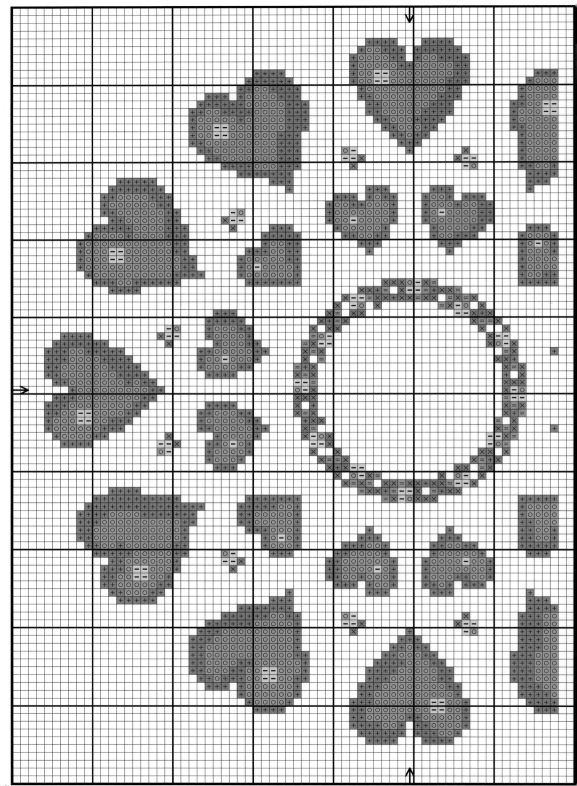

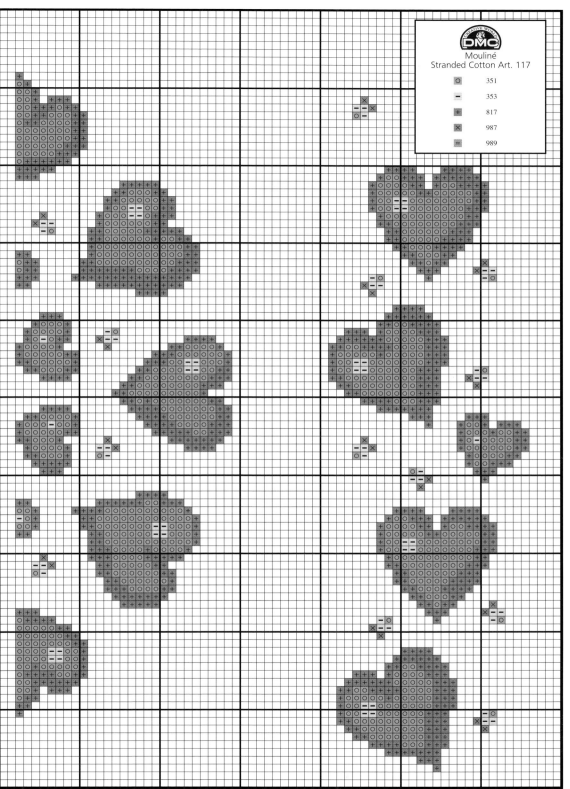

DMC
CREATIVE WORLD
Mouliné
Stranded Cotton Art. 117

O	351
−	353
+	817
×	987
=	989

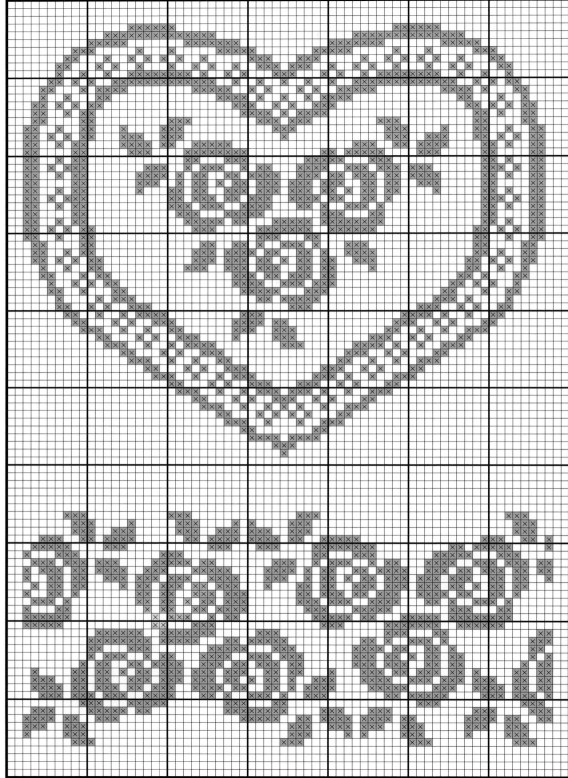

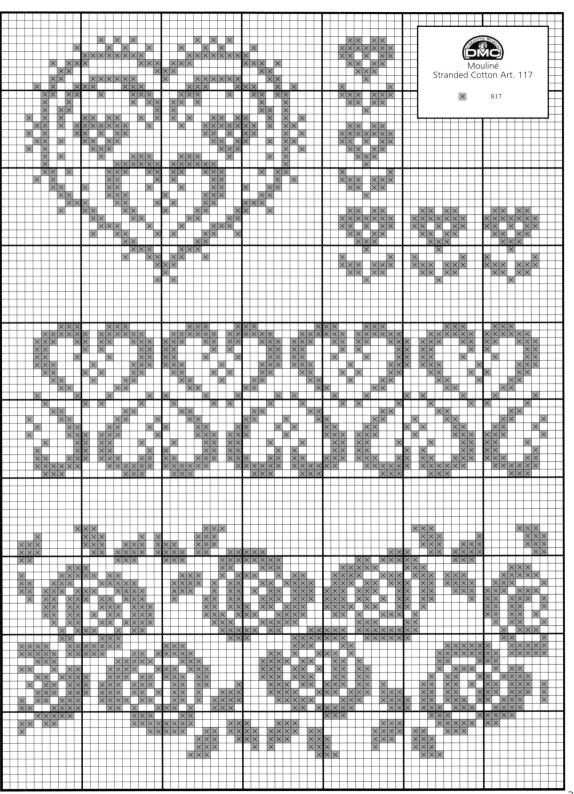

DMC
Mouliné
Stranded Cotton Art. 117

☒ 817

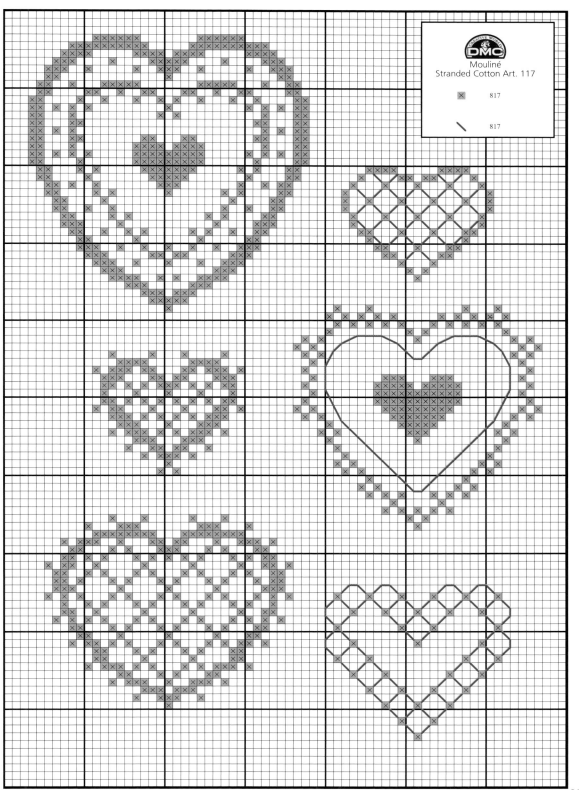

DMC
Mouliné
Stranded Cotton Art. 117

•	blanc	
+	ecru	
↑	351	
\	353	
⌐	434	
I	436	
U	498	
Z	518	
△	644	
O	676	
S	677	
–	741	
N	743	
≡	817	
▢	988	
×	3761	
3	3842	

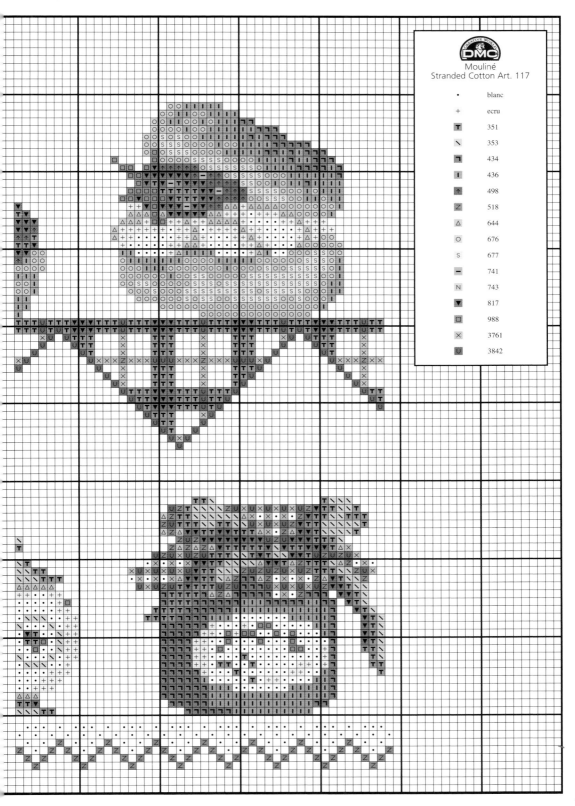

DMC
Mouliné
Stranded Cotton Art. 117

·	blanc	
+	ecru	
T	351	
\	353	
⌐	434	
I	436	
↑	498	
Z	518	
△	644	
O	676	
S	677	
–	741	
N	743	
▼	817	
□	988	
×	3761	
U	3842	

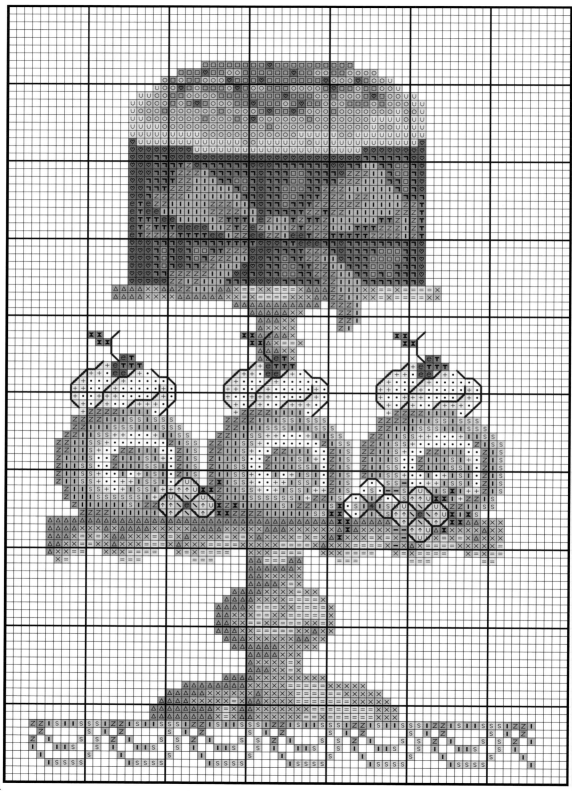

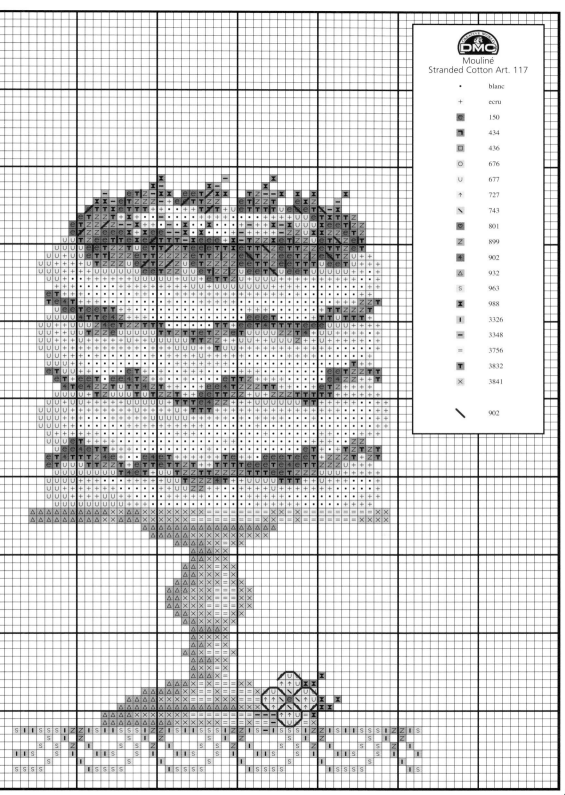

	DMC
	Mouliné Stranded Cotton Art. 117
•	blanc
+	ecru
⌼	150
◣	434
▢	436
○	676
U	677
↑	727
＼	743
⬙	801
Z	899
◹	902
△	932
S	963
✕	988
I	3326
—	3348
=	3756
T	3832
✕	3841
＼	902

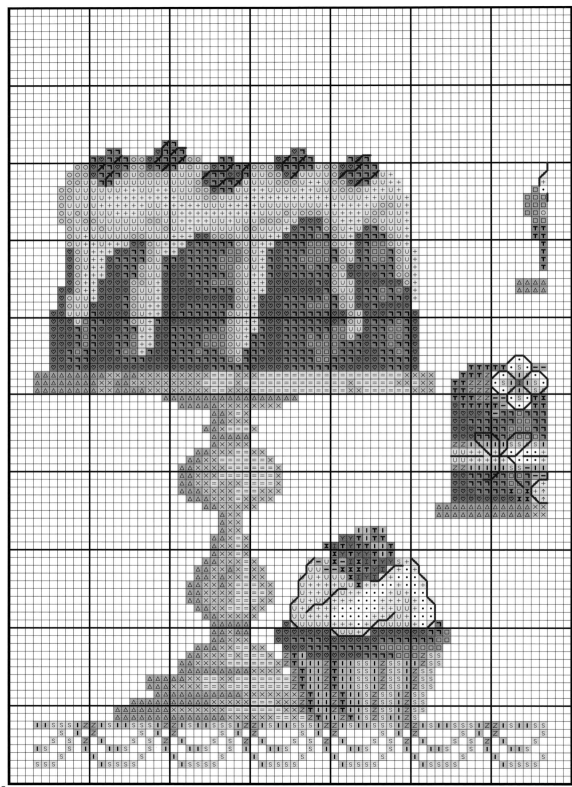

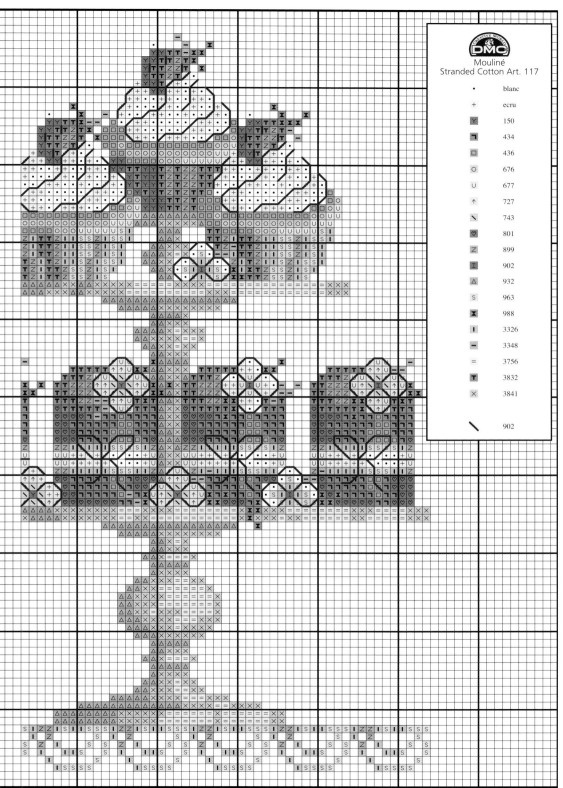

DMC
Mouliné
Stranded Cotton Art. 117

Symbol	Color
•	blanc
+	ecru
Y	150
⌐	434
□	436
O	676
U	677
↑	727
\	743
♡	801
Z	899
I	902
△	932
S	963
X	988
I	3326
—	3348
=	3756
T	3832
✕	3841
\	902

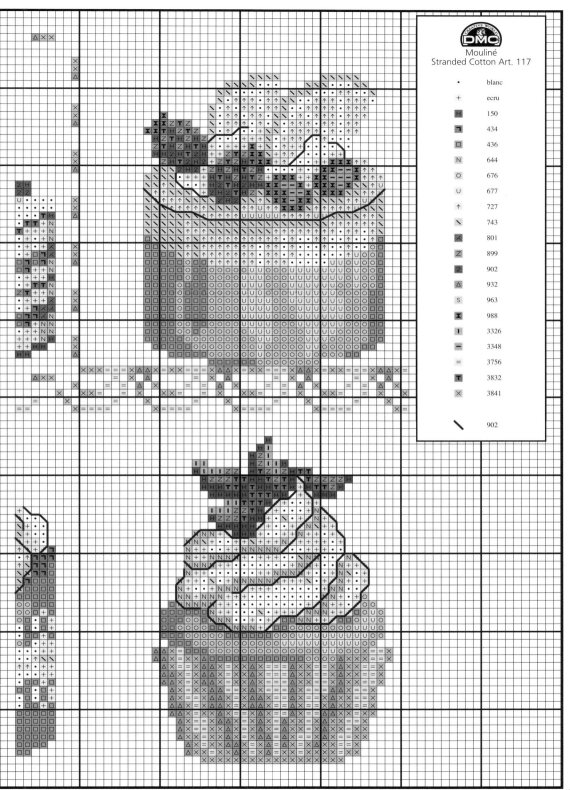

Symbol	Code
•	blanc
+	ecru
H	150
⌐	434
□	436
N	644
O	676
U	677
↑	727
\	743
⊠	801
Z	899
◩	902
△	932
S	963
⊠	988
I	3326
−	3348
=	3756
T	3832
X	3841
\	902

DMC
Mouliné
Stranded Cotton Art. 117

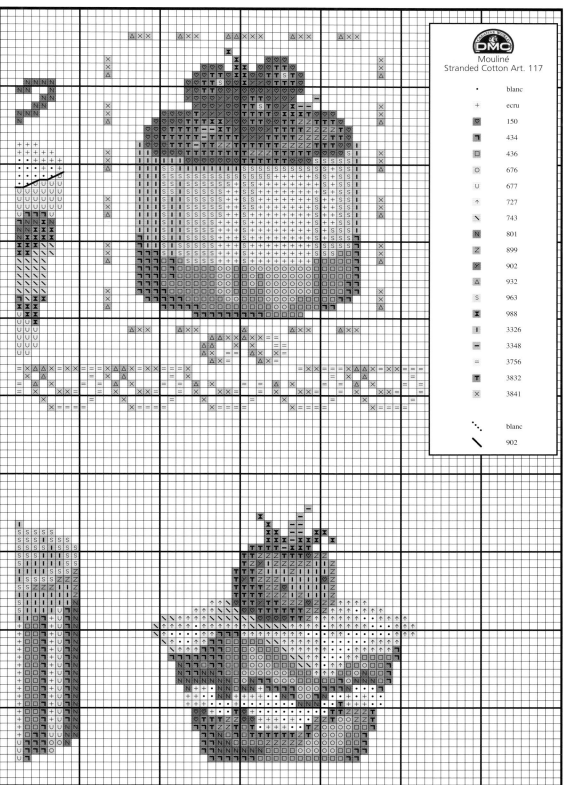

DMC
Mouliné
Stranded Cotton Art. 117

·	blanc
+	ecru
♡	150
⊐	434
▢	436
○	676
U	677
↑	727
＼	743
N	801
Z	899
✕	902
△	932
S	963
✗	988
I	3326
−	3348
=	3756
T	3832
✕	3841
⋰	blanc
╲	902

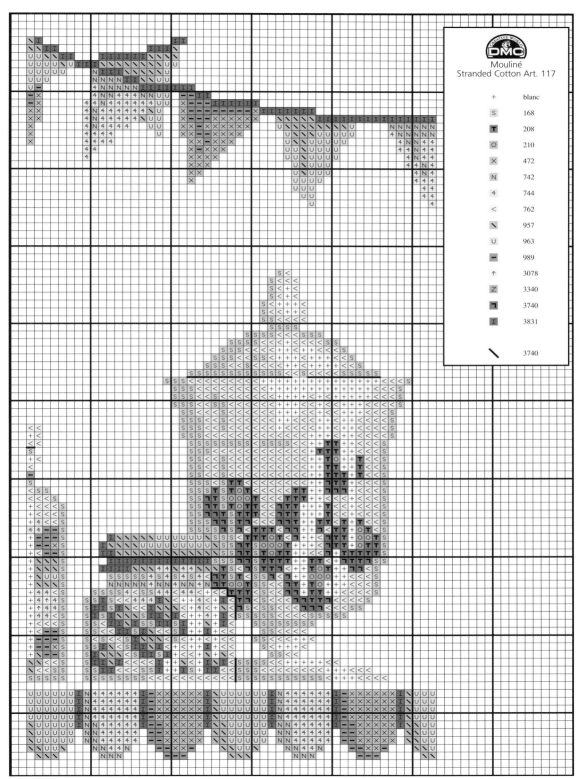

Mouliné
Stranded Cotton Art. 117

+	blanc
S	168
T	208
O	210
X	472
N	742
4	744
<	762
\	957
U	963
−	989
↑	3078
Z	3340
⌐	3740
I	3831
\	3740

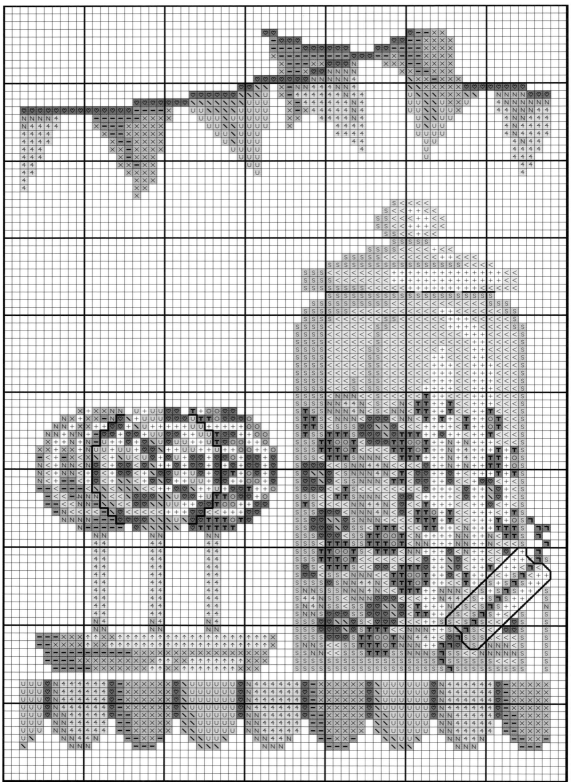

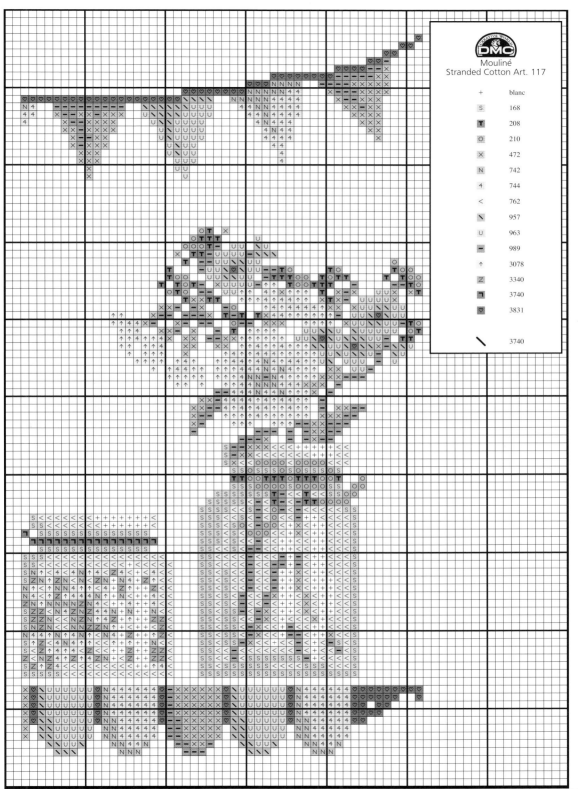

DMC
Mouliné
Stranded Cotton Art. 117

+	blanc
S	168
T	208
O	210
X	472
N	742
4	744
<	762
\	957
U	963
–	989
↑	3078
Z	3340
⌐	3740
♥	3831
\	3740

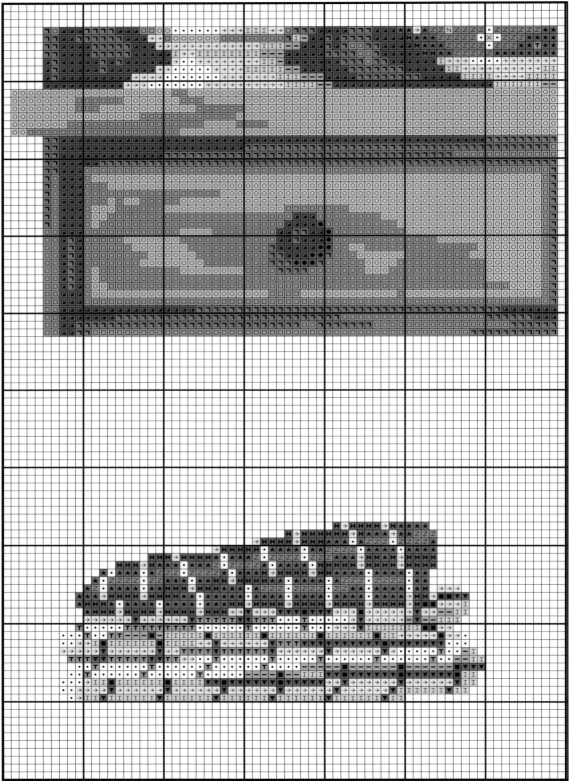

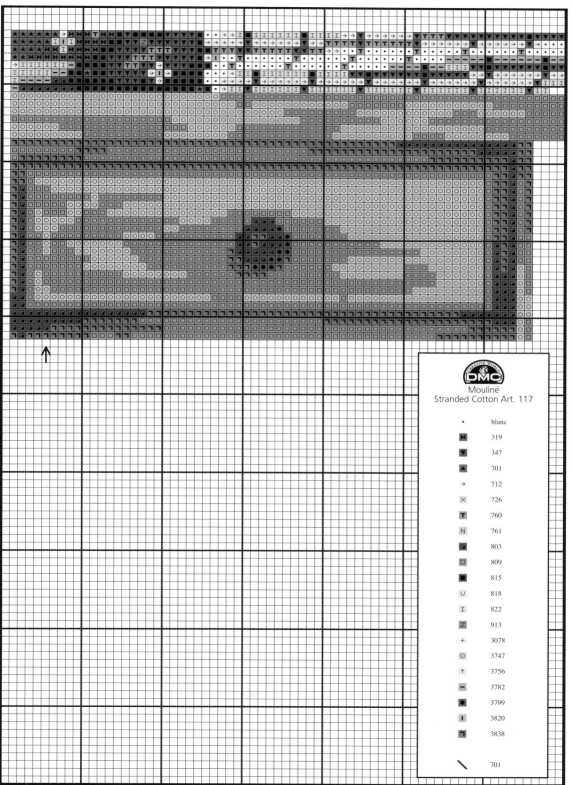

•	blanc
⋈	319
▼	347
★	701
→	712
×	726
T	760
N	761
▣	803
▢	809
■	815
U	818
I	822
Z	913
+	3078
O	3747
↑	3756
–	3782
●	3799
I	3820
⌐	3838
╲	701

Mouliné
Stranded Cotton Art. 117

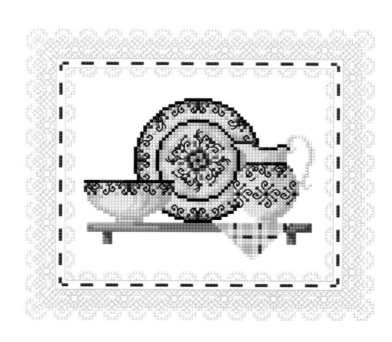

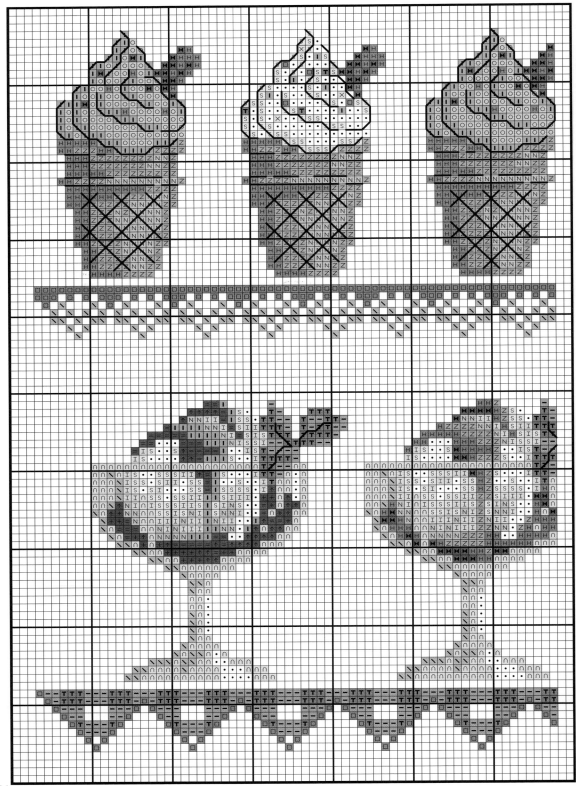

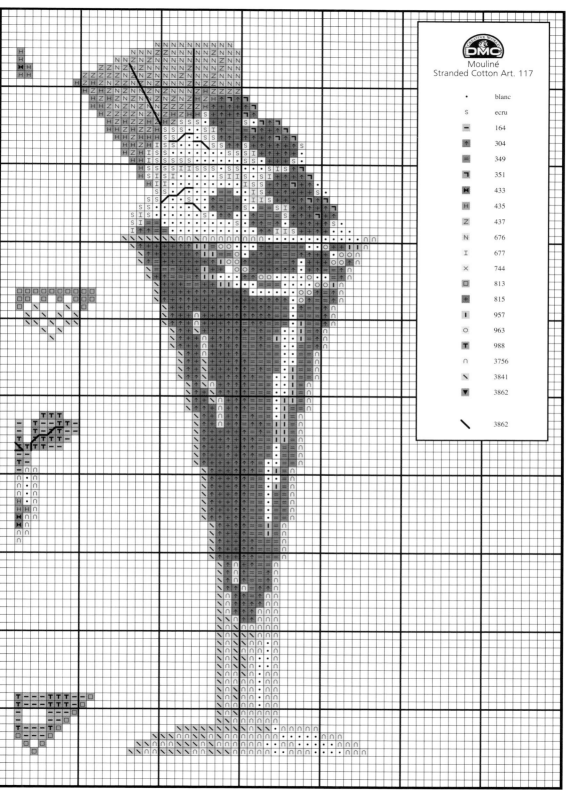

DMC
Mouliné
Stranded Cotton Art. 117

•	blanc	
S	ecru	
–	164	
↑	304	
=	349	
⌐	351	
⋈	433	
H	435	
Z	437	
N	676	
I	677	
×	744	
▢	813	
+	815	
I	957	
○	963	
T	988	
∩	3756	
＼	3841	
▼	3862	
＼	3862	

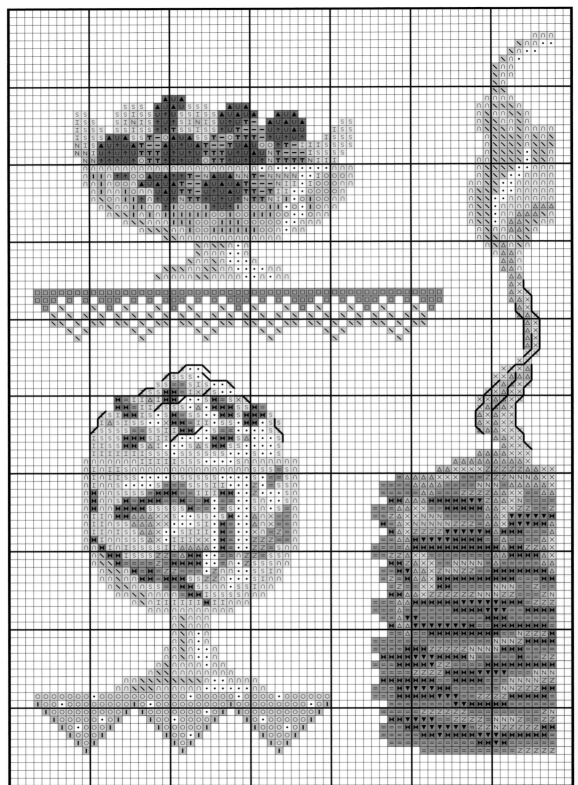

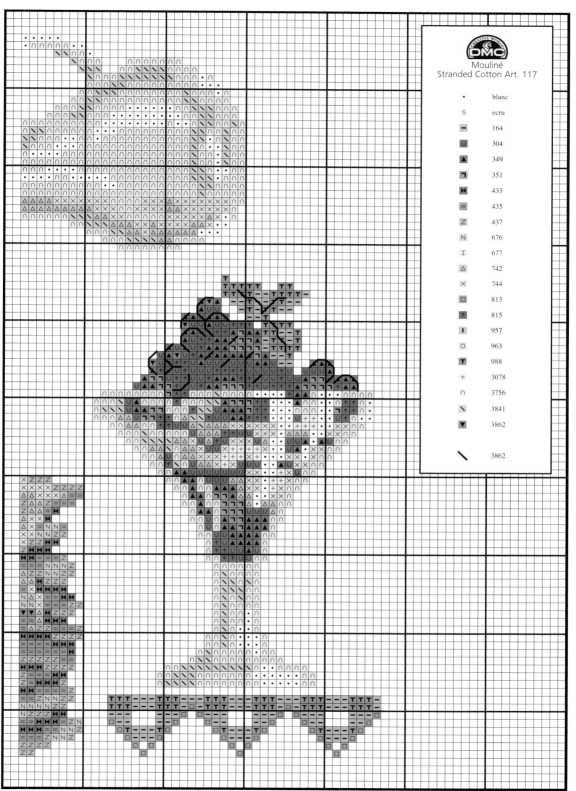

DMC
Mouliné
Stranded Cotton Art. 117

•	blanc
S	ecru
−	164
U	304
▲	349
⌐	351
⋈	433
=	435
Z	437
N	676
I	677
△	742
×	744
□	813
↑	815
I	957
o	963
T	988
+	3078
∩	3756
＼	3841
▼	3862
＼	3862

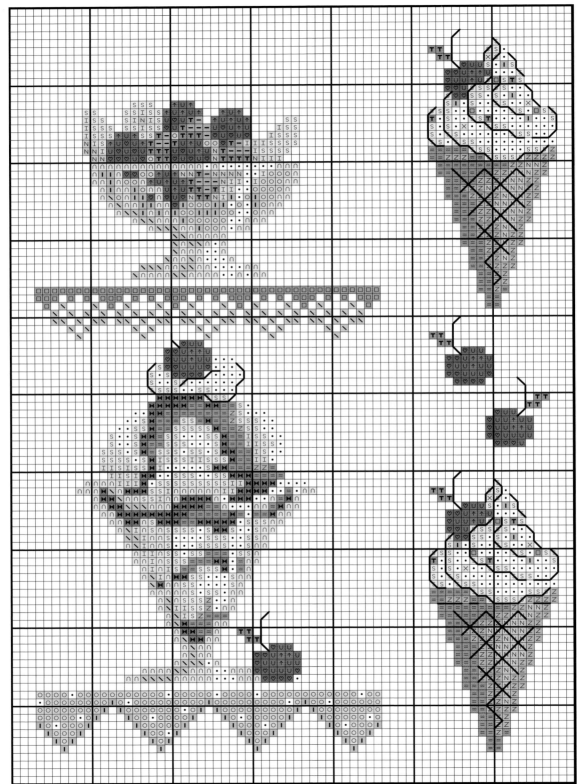

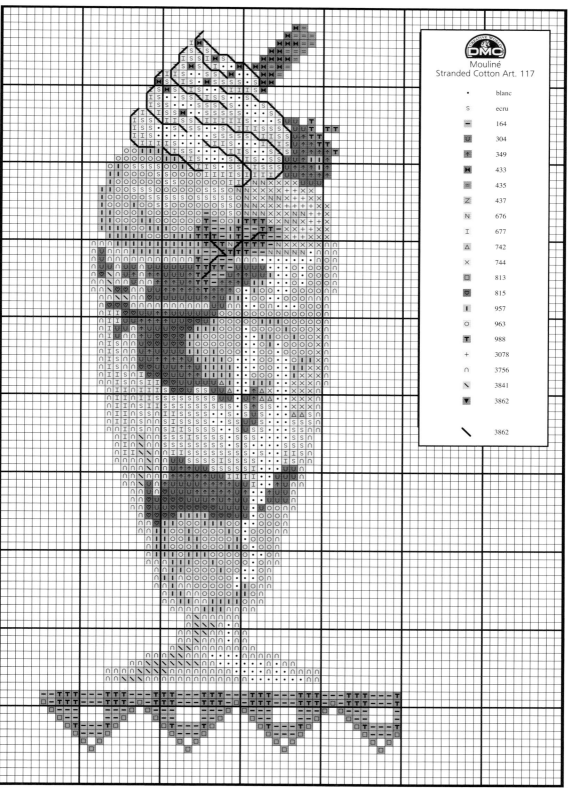

Mouliné
Stranded Cotton Art. 117

•	blanc
S	ecru
−	164
U	304
↑	349
ᴴ	433
≡	435
Z	437
N	676
I	677
△	742
×	744
□	813
♥	815
I	957
O	963
T	988
+	3078
∩	3756
\	3841
▼	3862
╲	3862

DMC
Mouliné
Stranded Cotton Art. 117

•	blanc
+	ecru
✗	347
T	351
Z	414
∩	415
★	434
△	436
▢	518
✕	676
S	677
╲	738
I	741
O	743
U	762
◢	823
◥	987
▬	989
‖	3078
N	3348
◣	3685
I	3761
▼	3842
	ecru
╲	823

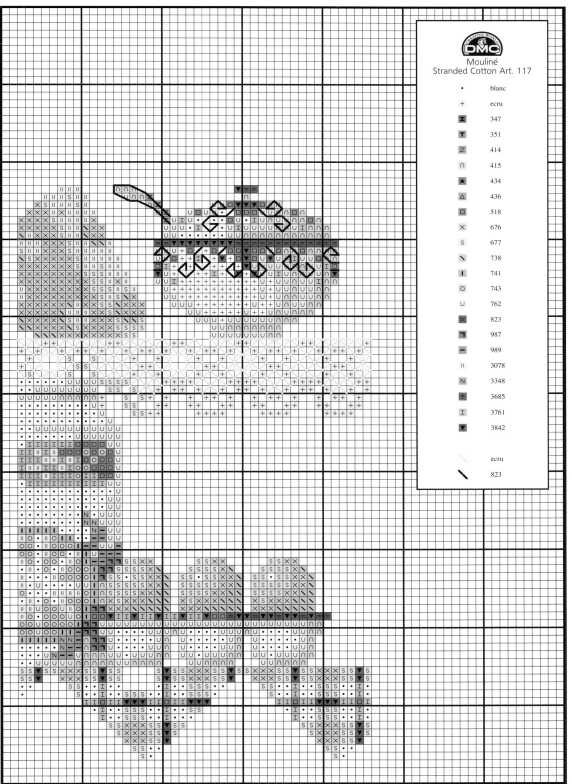

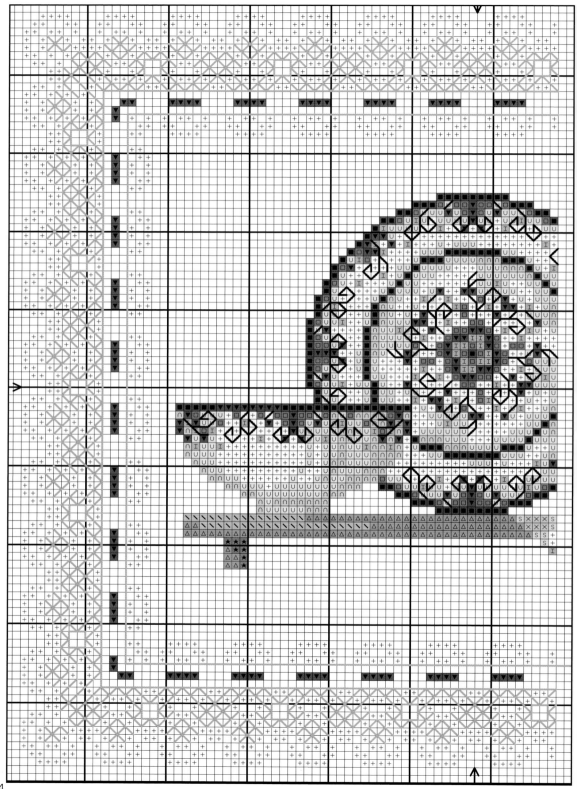

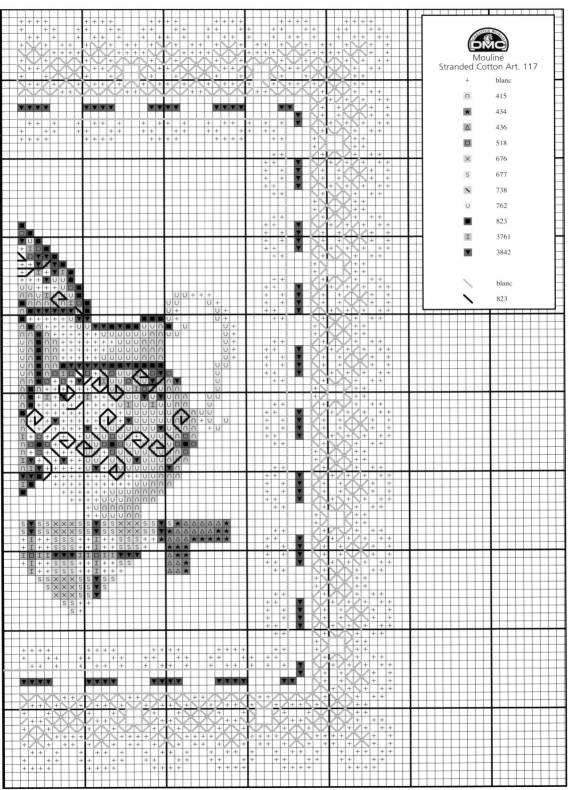

DMC
Mouliné
Stranded Cotton Art. 117

Symbol	Color
+	blanc
∩	415
★	434
△	436
⬜	518
✕	676
S	677
⟍	738
U	762
⬛	823
I	3761
▼	3842
⟍	blanc
⟍	823

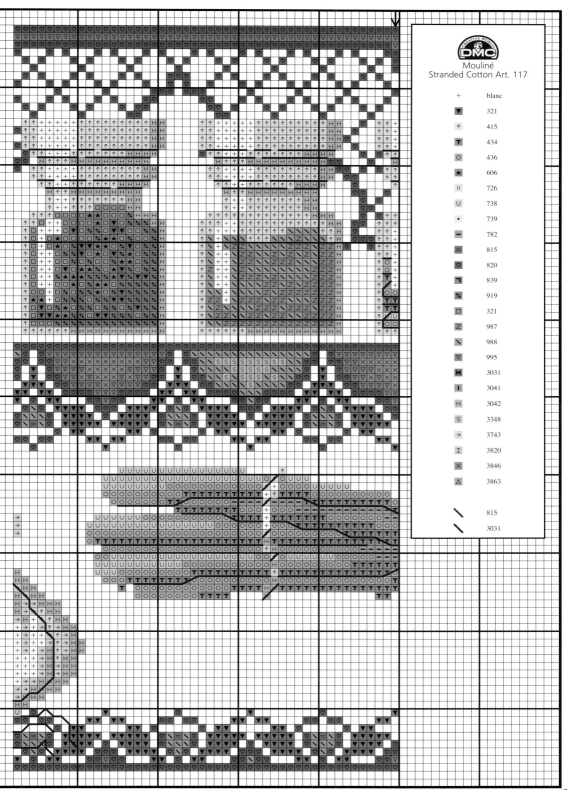

+	blanc
▼	321
↑	415
T	434
O	436
★	606
‖	726
U	738
•	739
−	782
●	815
4	820
⌐	839
%	919
□	921
Z	987
＼	988
▽	995
✕	3031
I	3041
H	3042
S	3348
→	3743
I	3820
✕	3846
△	3863
＼	815
＼	3031

DMC
Mouliné
Stranded Cotton Art. 117

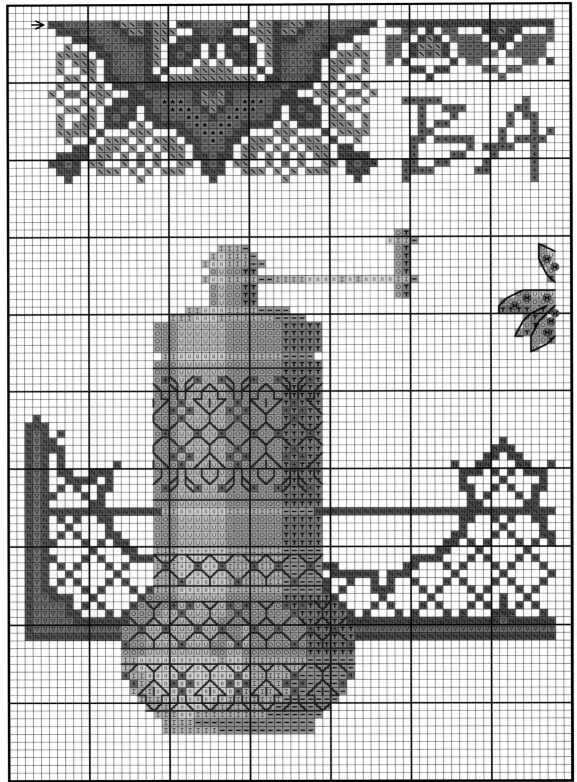

DMC
CREATIVE WORLD
Mouliné
Stranded Cotton Art. 117

Symbol	Colour
+	blanc
=	321
↑	415
T	434
O	436
★	606
II	726
U	738
·	739
−	782
4	815
N	820
⌐	839
%	919
□	321
Z	987
\	988
▽	995
⋈	3031
I	3041
H	3042
S	3348
→	3743
I	3820
×	3846
△	3863
\	815
\	3031
⋈	3031

DMC
Mouliné
Stranded Cotton Art. 117

+	blanc
▼	321
↑	415
T	434
O	436
★	606
‖	726
U	738
•	739
—	782
A	815
✳	820
◥	839
≡	919
□	921
Z	987
◣	988
▽	995
⋈	3031
I	3041
H	3042
S	3348
→	3743
I	3820
✕	3846
△	3863
╲	815
╲	3031

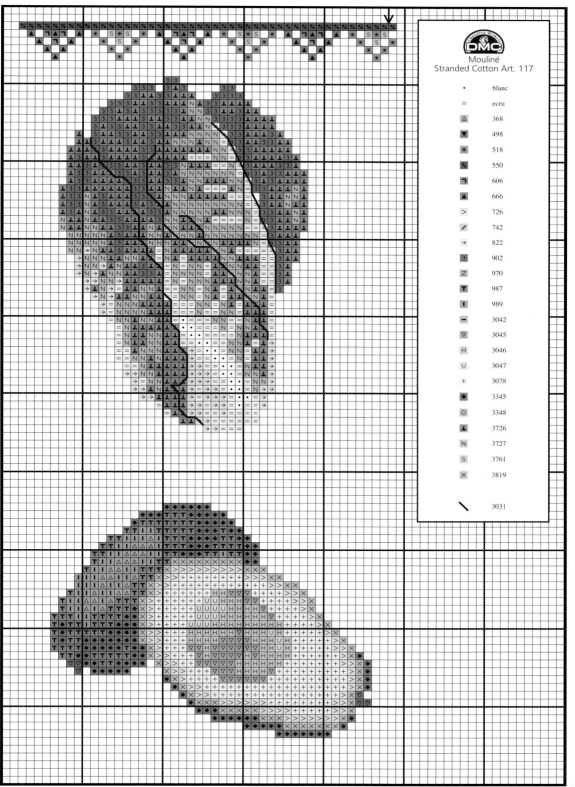

DMC
Mouliné
Stranded Cotton Art. 117

•	blanc
=	ecru
△	368
▼	498
✳	518
▨	550
⌐	606
▲	666
>	726
╱	742
→	822
3	902
Z	970
T	987
I	989
−	3042
▽	3045
H	3046
U	3047
+	3078
◆	3345
O	3348
⊥	3726
N	3727
S	3761
×	3819
╲	3031

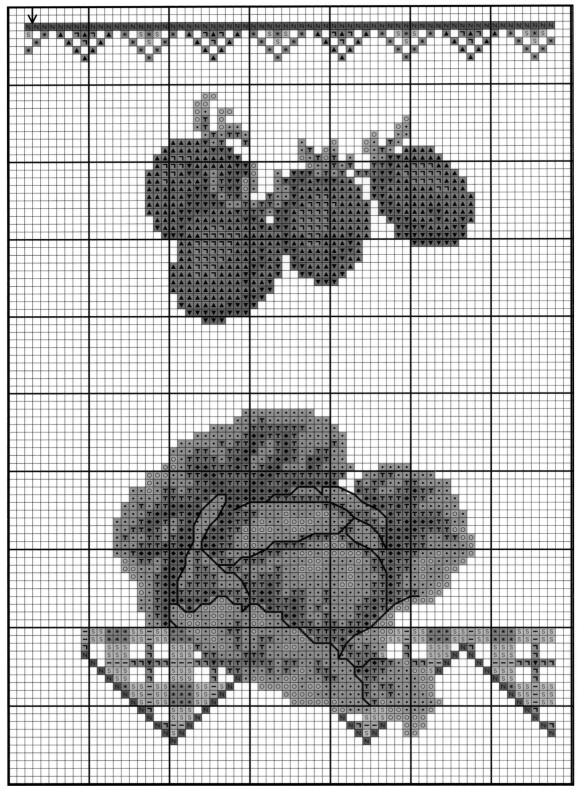

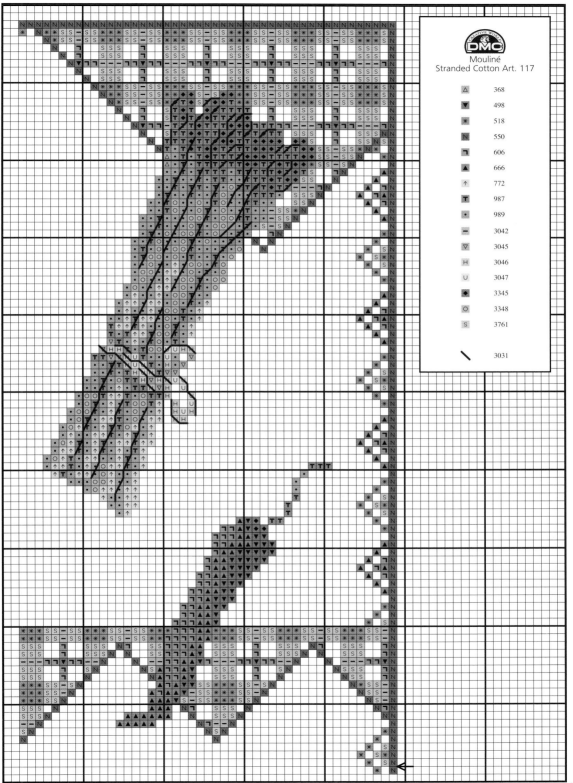

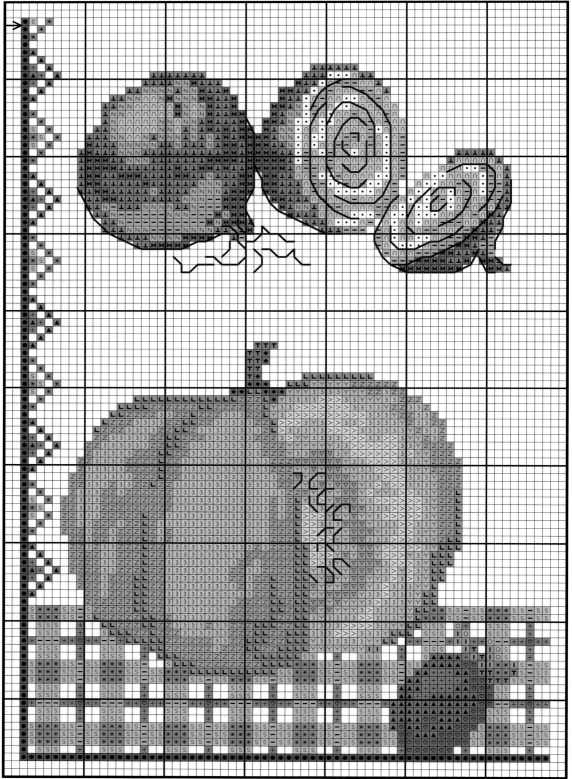

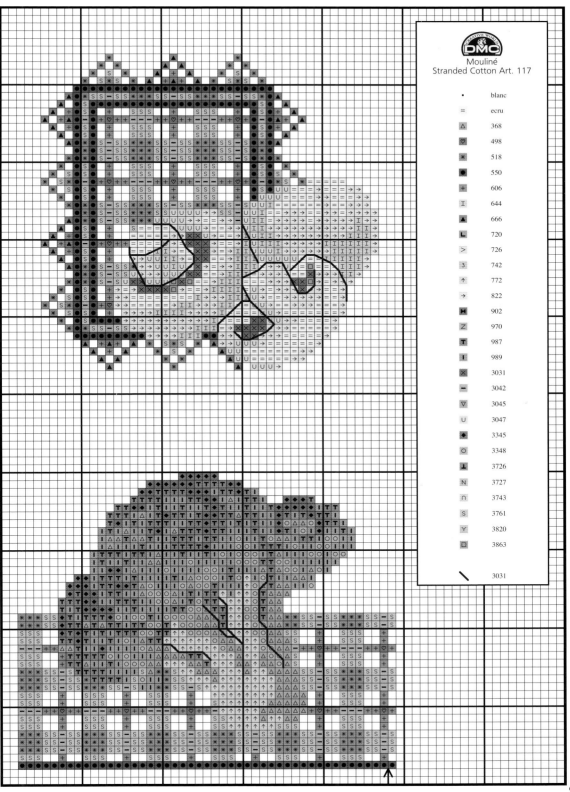

•	blanc	
=	ecru	
△	368	
♡	498	
✳	518	
●	550	
+	606	
I	644	
▲	666	
L	720	
>	726	
3	742	
↑	772	
→	822	
⊞	902	
Z	970	
T	987	
I	989	
✕	3031	
−	3042	
▽	3045	
U	3047	
◆	3345	
○	3348	
⊥	3726	
N	3727	
∩	3743	
S	3761	
Y	3820	
▢	3863	
╲	3031	

DMC
Mouliné
Stranded Cotton Art. 117

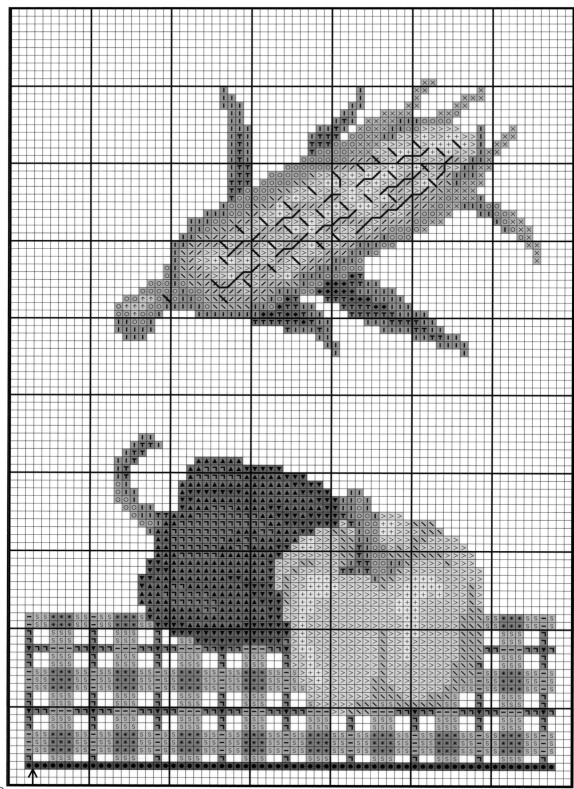

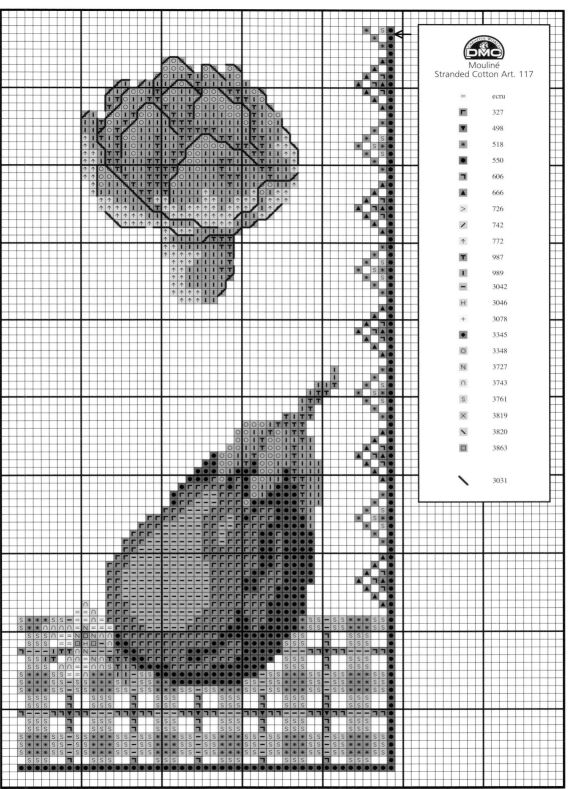

DMC
Mouliné
Stranded Cotton Art. 117

=	ecru
⌐	327
▼	498
✳	518
●	550
⌐	606
▲	666
>	726
∕	742
↑	772
T	987
I	989
−	3042
H	3046
+	3078
◆	3345
O	3348
N	3727
∩	3743
S	3761
×	3819
＼	3820
▢	3863
＼	3031

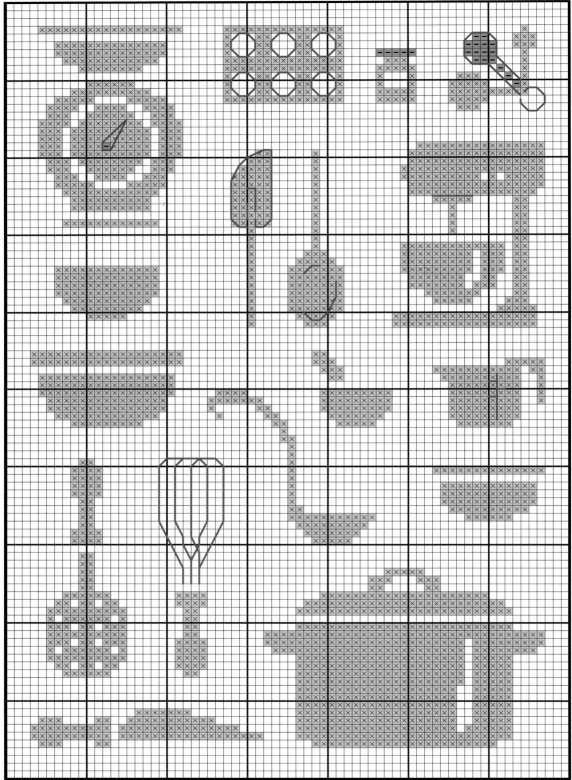

DMC
Mouliné
Stranded Cotton Art. 117

| — | 931 |
| × | 3841 |

/ 931

DMC
Mouliné
Stranded Cotton Art. 117

−	518
×	3761
•	3842

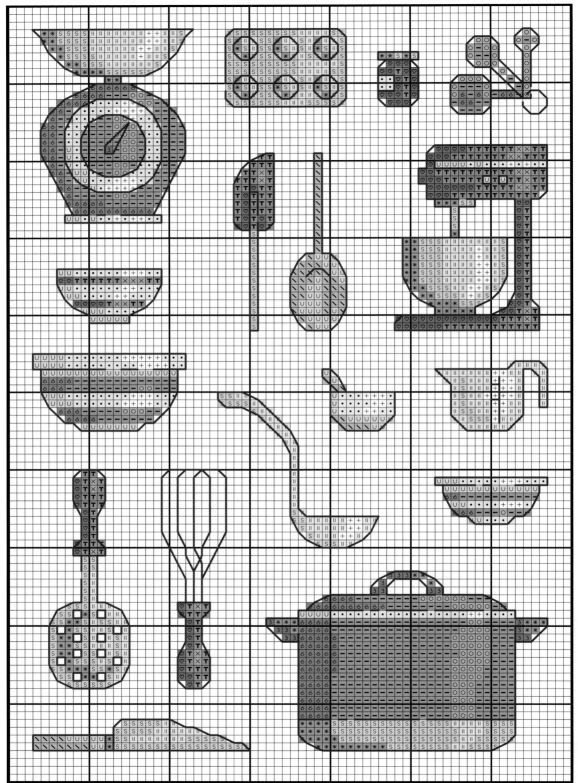

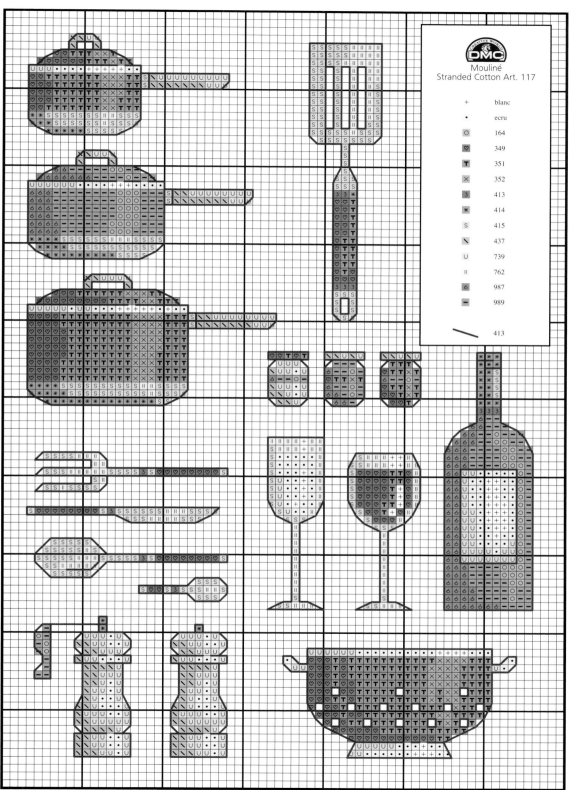

DMC
Mouliné
Stranded Cotton Art. 117

+		blanc
•		ecru
O		164
♡		349
T		351
✕		352
3		413
✻		414
S		415
╲		437
U		739
‖		762
૬		987
−		989
╱		413

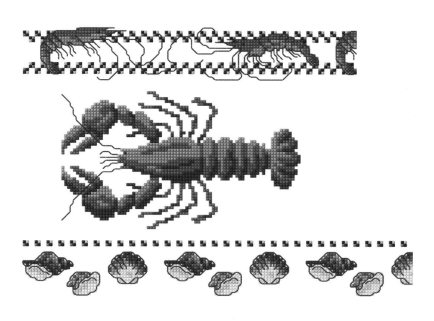

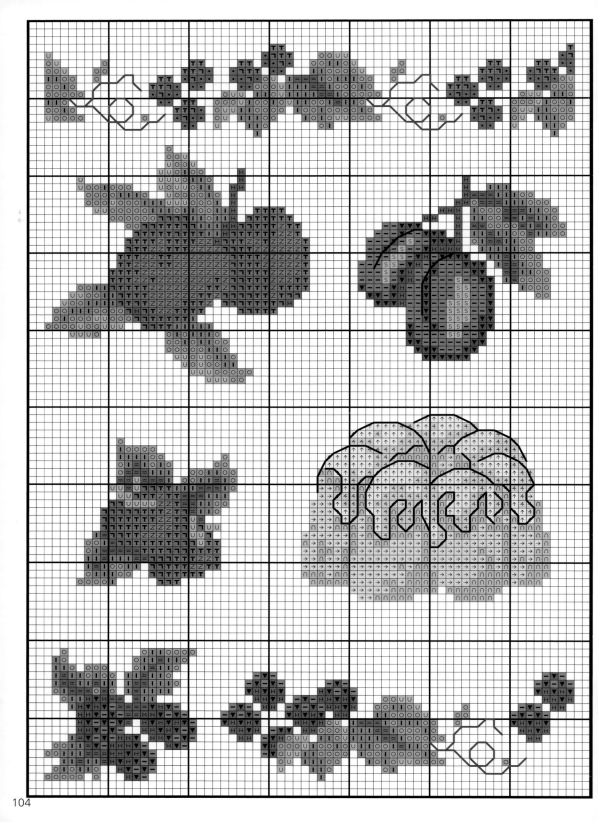

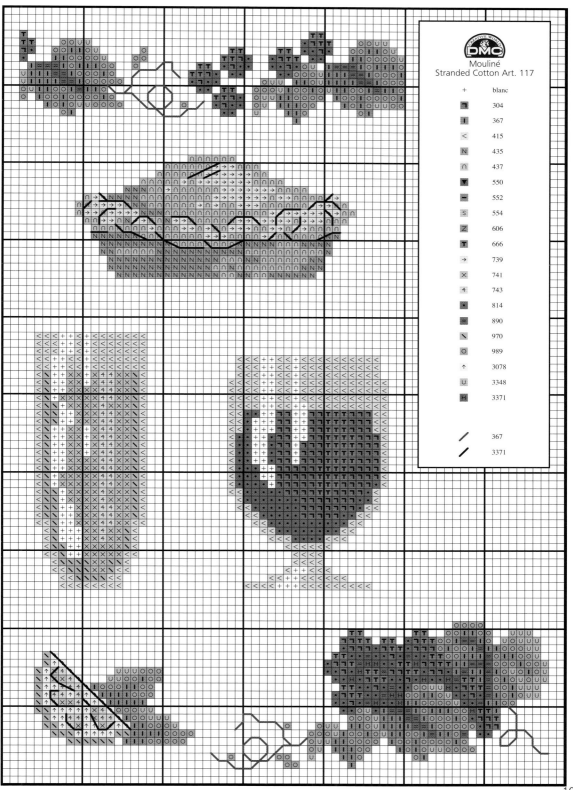

DMC
Mouliné
Stranded Cotton Art. 117

+	blanc
⌐	304
I	367
<	415
N	435
∩	437
▼	550
━	552
S	554
Z	606
T	666
→	739
✕	741
✦	743
•	814
≡	890
↘	970
O	989
↑	3078
U	3348
H	3371
╱	367
╱	3371

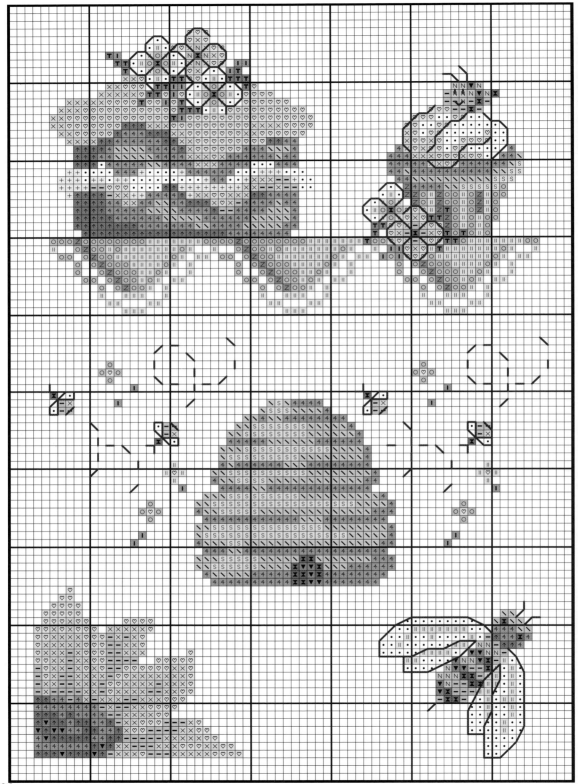

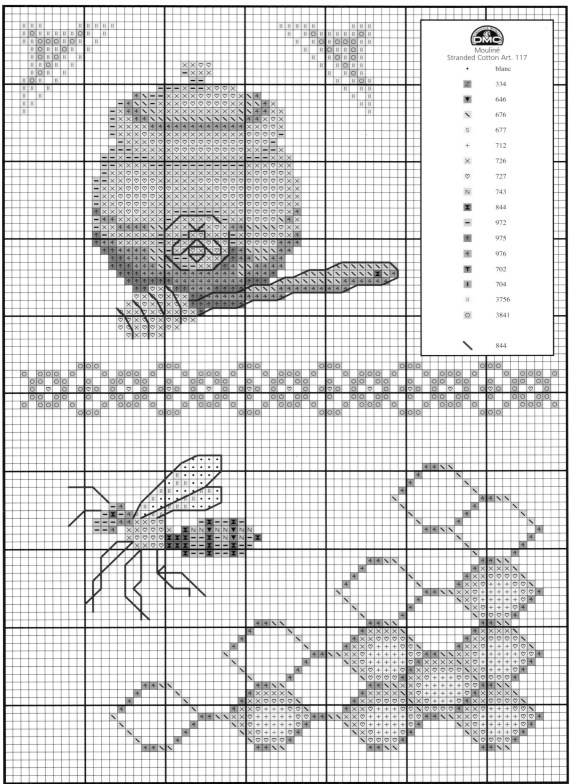

DMC
Mouliné
Stranded Cotton Art. 117

•	blanc
Z	334
▼	646
╲	676
S	677
+	712
✕	726
♡	727
N	743
✕	844
−	972
↑	975
4	976
T	702
I	704
II	3756
O	3841
╲	844

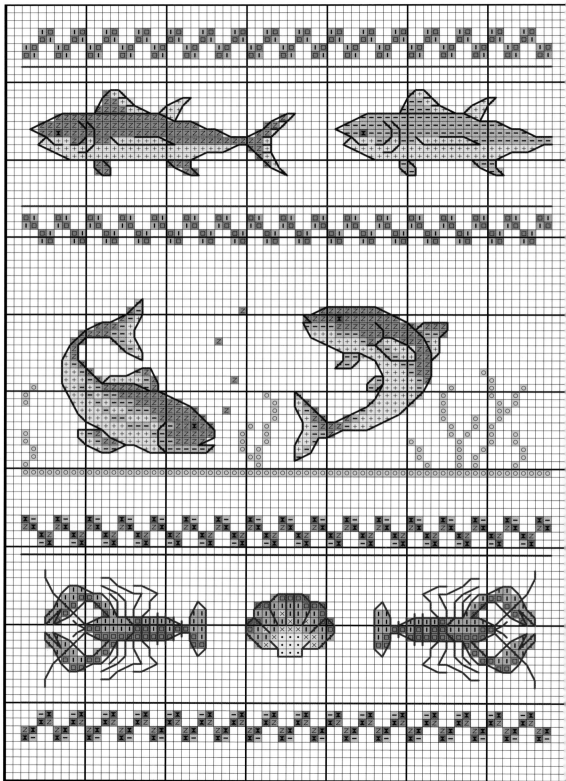

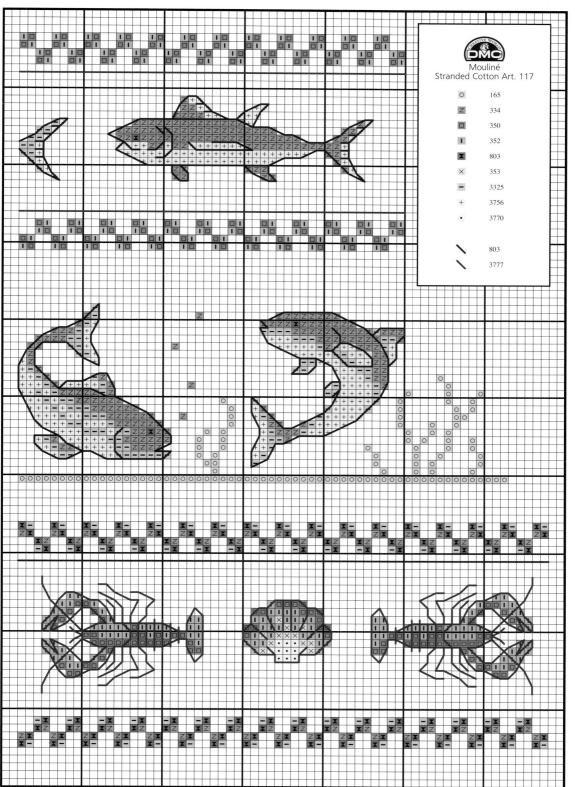

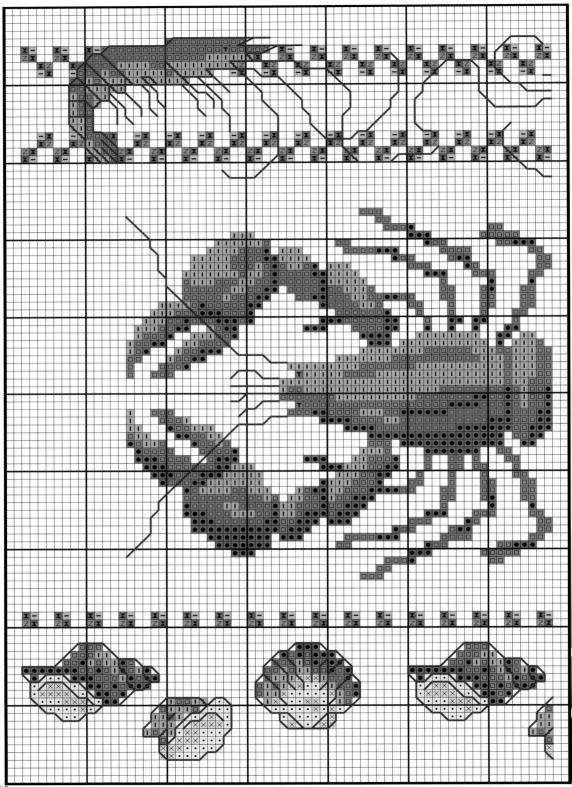